# INTRODUCTION

## Hello and welcome to the Roblox Annual 2020!

My name is Dave, though you might know me better as Builderman. I'm one of the original creators of Roblox and I'll be your guide through this wonderful world of ours. Whether this is your first time exploring Roblox or you've contributed your own creations before, you'll find within these pages a bounty of knowledge and inspiration from our amazing community.

Roblox is a place that's built entirely by you. These are your stories, your adventures, your characters, your experiences. This book is a celebration of everything that you and millions of other Robloxians have helped create. We'll look at some of the most popular games on Roblox, meet famous developers and creators from the community, check out our massive Bloxy Awards ceremony and so much more.

Turn the page and let's embark on another exciting adventure inside the world of Roblox!

Sincerely,
**David Baszucki, a.k.a. Builderman**

# ROBLOX RETROSPECTIVE

*It's been another super-busy twelve months on Roblox. Tons of new games, records smashed, useful tools developed – the list goes on! Take a look at some of the key stories from this year.*

## TOP OF THE CHARTS

Roblox is obviously awesome, but now it's officially the top online entertainment platform for kids and teens. Roblox has over 90 million monthly users and this number continues to grow! The success is down to the amazing community of devs and gamers who make the site what it is, plus all the cool social interactivity that Robloxians enjoy.

## LOCO FOR LOCALISATION

Roblox has global appeal, so now it's easier for developers to localise their games and change text for players who speak other languages. New tools in Roblox Studio make it simple for devs to localise games and reach a wider audience.

## ACCELERATED DEVELOPMENT

As they do every year, the folks at Roblox welcomed an influx of developers to Roblox HQ as part of its Incubator and Accelerator programs. Participants get to work at Roblox, collaborate with peers and create awesome games. You can already play some of their creations, like Ventureland and Robot 64.

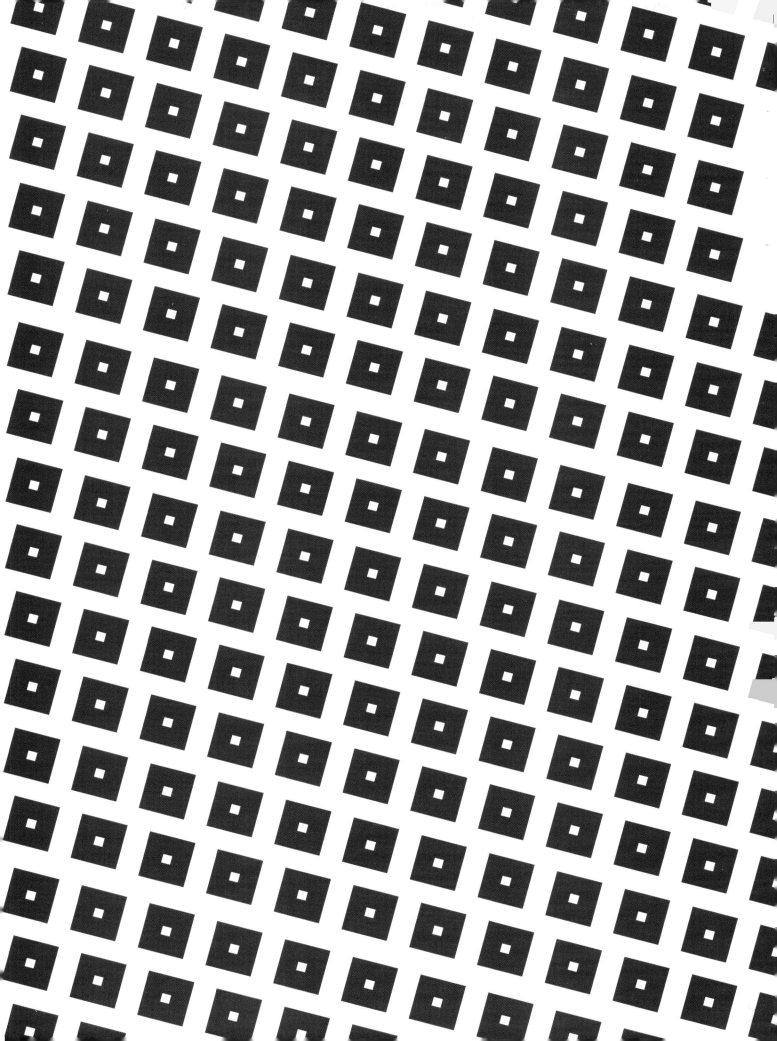

# EGMONT

*We bring stories to life*

First published in Great Britain 2019, by Egmont UK Limited
The Yellow Building, 1 Nicholas Road
London W11 4AN

Written by Andy Davidson and Craig Jelley
Edited by Craig Jelley
Designed by John Stuckey and Ian Pollard
Illustrations by John Stuckey, Ryan Marsh and Isaac & Oscar Riordan
Special thanks to the entire Roblox team
Texture images: Shutterstock.com

All statistics featured in this book were based on information publicly available
on the Roblox platform and were correct as of March 2019.

ISBN 978 1 4052 9445 4

70368/005
Printed in Italy

Spending time online is great fun! Here are a few simple rules to help younger fans stay safe and keep
the internet a great place to hang out. For more advice and guidance, please see page 68 of this
book, or go to www.connectsafely.org/Roblox

- Never give out your real name – don't use it as your username.
- Never give out any of your personal details.
- Never tell anybody which school you go to or how old you are.
- Never tell anybody your password except a parent or guardian.
- Be aware that you must be 13 or over to create an account on many sites. Always check
the site policy and ask a parent or guardian for permission before registering.
- Always tell a parent or guardian if something is worrying you.

Stay safe online. Any website addresses listed in this book are correct at the time of going to print.
However, Egmont is not responsible for content hosted by third parties. Please be aware that online
content can be subject to change and websites can contain content that is unsuitable for children.
We advise that all children are supervised when using the internet.

Egmont takes its responsibility to the planet and its inhabitants very seriously.
We aim to use papers from well-managed forests run by responsible suppliers.

# ROBLOX

## ANNUAL 2020

# CONTENTS

## ROBLOX STUDIO DARK THEME
Developers lovingly create their games at all hours of the day. To make it a bit easier on the night owls' eyes, Roblox introduced a dark theme for Roblox Studio. It changes all the light areas on the screen to black, which makes it much easier to look at when the lights are low.

## WELL-EDUCATED
Not content with being the most popular entertainment platform, Roblox released Roblox Education, a curriculum of resources aimed at increasing STEM knowledge using Roblox. Whether you want to learn or teach using Roblox as a tool, you can find out more by heading to *corp.roblox.com/education*

## TOY-TASTIC!
Robloxian characters continue to migrate from the virtual world to the real one, and there are new series available in a toy shop near you! They feature characters from some of Roblox's biggest games and are perfect for adding to your collection. There are more than toys on the way too – watch out for cool apparel and even more amazing books on the shelves!

9

# PARTY TIME

*Roblox is full of ways you can connect and play with your real-life friends. From simply chatting to jumping into games and starting groups, there are so many ways to buddy up and play!*

## GET STARTED!

The first thing you need to do is add some friends. This is easy; just type your buddy's username into the search bar. Once you've found them, click on the name to see their user profile. Select Add Friend and you're done!

## FRIEND REQUESTS

Check out who's in your Friends list by clicking Friends to the right of your username. If your real-life pal has sent you a friend request, it will appear here. Simply click to confirm or reject the request.

## BEST FRIENDS!

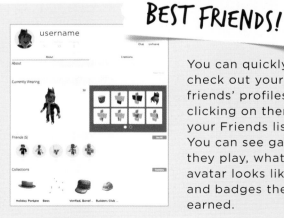

You can quickly check out your friends' profiles by clicking on them in your Friends list. You can see games they play, what their avatar looks like and badges they've earned.

# GET CHATTING!

The simplest way to chat with friends is from the home screen. Just click the blue chat bar on the bottom right-hand corner of the page to bring up your friends list. Click on someone to get chatting!

# SAFE SOCIALISING

Roblox is a fun and safe place to play, but like anywhere on the internet you should be sensible in how you use it. Here are some tips for looking after yourself and your account:

■ Be careful who you add as a friend. Don't accept friend requests from strangers.

■ Use the Report Abuse feature if anyone is abusive or tries to scam you with something like free Robux.

■ Keep your personal details secret, including your name, address and date of birth.

■ For more tips on staying safe in Roblox, check out the guide on page 68.

# GROUP CHAT

To chat with more than one of your friends at a time, just create a group. Click Create Group Chat and add any friends you want to have in the group.

# PLAY TOGETHER

Easily find out what your friends are doing by taking a look at your chat box. The game that each friend is playing will appear next to their username. If Join appears next to the game just hit it to jump into the same game.

# GAME AND CHAT

You can chat in-game too. Just hit the '/' key to bring up the chat box and talk to people playing the same game. This is a great way to communicate with friends while playing.

## TIP!

Change the name of your group chat by clicking the gear icon at the top of the chat box and selecting Chat Group Name. Call it anything you like!

11

# TOP 10 MOST-PLAYED GAMES ON ROBLOX

*There are hundreds of games vying for attention on Roblox, and some reach dizzy heights of popularity. This top ten celebrates those that have made it to the top, beginning with unusual games about digs and tribes.*

## 10

## TREASURE HUNT SIMULATOR

Grab your shovel and dig in with Treasure Hunt Simulator. It's a race to the bottom of the pit as everyone makes their way through the layers of sand, hunting for coins and treasure. All your earnings can be reinvested in your tools so that you can dig your way down even faster.

### THE DIG BEGINS

You'll start the game with just a bucket and a small backpack. The bucket will pick up one lot of sand at a time, and your backpack can only hold ten lots of sand before you need to sell it at the store. At the top of the dig site, each block will be made of 5 sand, so it will be a slow process to begin with.

### BURIED TREASURE

As you dig deeper and deeper, you'll find chests buried in the sand. Each one will reward you with coins and gems that you can use in the shop.

### EQUIPMENT UPGRADE

You can invest the gold you've earned in different items that will increase your productivity. Backpacks have increased storage so you can dig for longer without returning to the surface, while certain tools will allow you to dig more quickly. You can also get cosmetic skins for your tools and pets that follow you around and help you out!

### DEVELOPER
**HenryDev**
*Over 250 million visitors have played Treasure Hunt Simulator, made by the creative HenryDev.*

# BOOGA BOOGA

In prehistoric times there's a fine line between survival and death! BOOGA BOOGA by Soybeen lets you experience the life of a hunter-gatherer yourself. Set on a range of islands with varying terrains, there's loads to discover and do. Form a tribe, build a home and collect cool weapons and armour.

## SNOW WAY!

When you start the game, you only have a single possession: a rock. This limited tool lets you slowly chop down trees and defend yourself from attack. Your priority should be to explore your immediate area and grab any resources you can. Hit everything with your rock! You'll soon level up and get the recipes you need to make better equipment.

## TRIBAL LIFE

In BOOGA BOOGA you have the ability to form tribes. You can invite other players to join your tribe so you can pool resources and power to get things done. Try raiding another camp or work together to smash one of the many god-heads that are dotted across the islands.

## DEVELOPER

### Soybeen

*BOOGA BOOGA dev Soybeen also created the games BIG BOOGA DIG, Dusk and Dawn.*

## EARLY LIFE FORMS

Humans aren't alone in this strange land. You'll find all sorts of native life wandering around, from the woolly mammoth and unusual insectoid antmen to the gigantic ... giants. They're a sight to behold but be wary around all of them. They're trying to survive too!

# ROBLOX CREATOR CHALLENGE – PART 1

*You may have played the best games on Roblox, but have you ever tried to create your own? If not, don't worry – we're here to give you a headstart on making your first game in Studio. These pages will explain how to set up your Place in order to start making your game.*

**1** When you download Roblox, you'll receive access to Roblox Studio, which is what creators use to make all your favourite games on the Roblox platform. Find the blue Roblox icon and double click it to open Studio.

**2** When Studio opens, you'll be presented with a number of templates to choose from. For the purpose of this walkthrough, we'll be using the 'baseplate' template, but pick the one you like most.

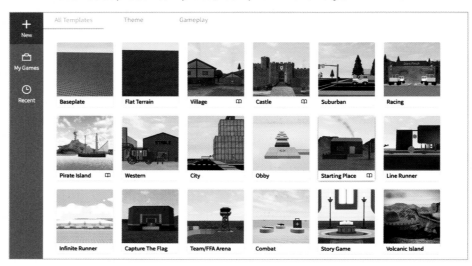

**3** You'll be taken to the Studio interface. In the centre you'll see the baseplate, where you'll do the majority of your game creation. You'll also notice some windows around the edges – Toolbox displays models you can use in your game, Explorer shows every object that appears in the game scene, and the Properties tab shows data relating to these objects. You can toggle them on and off in the View menu at the top of the screen.

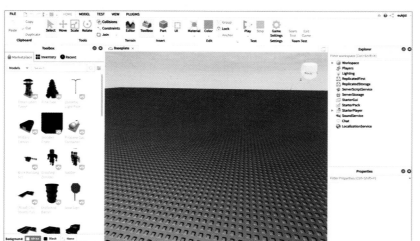

**4** To begin, you'll need to place an object to determine where players will spawn. Right click on Workspace and click 'Insert Object', then find the object called 'Spawn Location'. You'll see an object has been added to the Workspace section of the Explorer. Rename it to 'SpawnPoint1'.

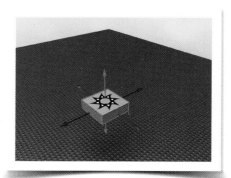

**5** Now the SpawnPoint is in your game world, you can alter it however you like. Just be careful that you don't set it at such an angle that you'll fall off as soon as you spawn. Select the SpawnPoint, then use one of the manipulation options to change it:

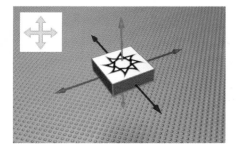

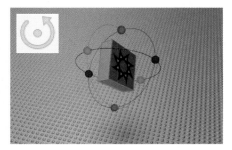

**MOVE:** Allows you to move the SpawnPoint's position in the game world.

**SCALE:** Lets you increase or decrease the width, length or height of the SpawnPoint.

**ROTATE:** Rotates the SpawnPoint along an axis – handy for angled surfaces.

Move, scale and rotate the SpawnPoint in your game world until you're happy with how it appears. Note that you can use the same controls to alter any part in your game.

**6** Now make a rough course by copying the spawn points. Right click on SpawnPoint1 in the Explorer, then select Duplicate. Another part will appear in the Workspace and game window. Rename it 'SpawnPoint2' and move the piece around in the game window. Repeat this process two times to make a short obby course.

**7** Finally, we're going to turn the SpawnPoints into working checkpoints. Select SpawnPoint1 in the Explorer and its properties will be shown in the Properties tab. Scroll down until you find the Teams section. Uncheck the Neutral box, check the AllowTeamChangeOnTouch box, then choose a unique TeamColor. Make a note of the colour you chose.

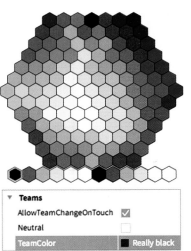

**8** Next, click the Model option at the top of the screen to bring up a new Toolbar, then press the Services button. Select Teams and a new option will appear in the Explorer. Right click on the Teams option, click Insert Object and then add a 'Team'. Rename the team to SpawnPoint1, then select it to bring up its properties. Change the TeamColor option to the same colour as the one you assigned to the SpawnPoint in the Workspace.

**9** Now repeat this for all the SpawnPoints you created. If you have four SpawnPoints, you should have four Teams. If you have ten SpawnPoints, then you should have ten Teams, and the corresponding TeamColor should be the same for the team and the SpawnPoint. Press the Play button and run between the checkpoints. In the corner of the screen, your username should switch between the named teams.

# GAMES YOU MAY HAVE MISSED

*With so many awesome games on Roblox, you'd be forgiven for letting a couple pass you by. We've collected a few hidden gems for your consideration. Here are the first pair to play!*

## FEED YOUR PETS

Feed Your Pets is an adventure farming game created by studio small games. As the name suggests, a key part of the game is keeping your cute critters well fed. Start by choosing a pet to come and live with you on your farm. The rest is up to you to discover.

### THE NEED FOR FEED

Your pet needs food and it's your job to get it! Grow food from seeds or scour the land looking for wild plants. Any money earned can be used to buy more seeds, gadgets or pet eggs to expand your collection!

### REALLY WILD PETS

Feed your pet to raise its level and unlock abilities, like being able to ride them! There are loads of animals in the game to discover and tame including lions, tigers, pigs, seagulls and even mythical, prehistoric and alien creatures!

## Developer
**small games**

small games is a new studio owned by Wheatlies, jameeish and Injanity. Feed Your Pets is the first game they've released together.

# Q-CLASH

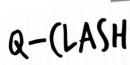

In Q-Clash, you can pick from eight unique hero classes and jump into a mission against an enemy team. Each class has different skills, which makes every match dynamic and unpredictable. Pick a character and jump right into the fray!

## PRIME OBJECTIVE

Every match is different – there are a handful of incredible levels to navigate and master. Each map has many areas to exploit to your character's advantage, and there are multiple objectives to complete too.

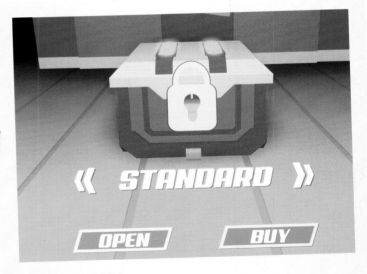

## LOOT HAPPY

As you defeat enemies, complete objectives and win matches, you'll gain experience and level up. When your level increases, you'll unlock a loot box, which will reward you with a random cosmetic item for one of the characters. If you can't wait to level up, you can use gems to purchase more boxes.

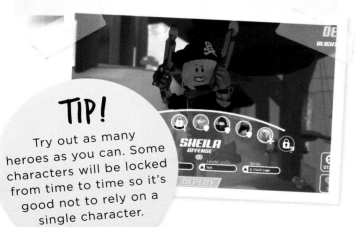

## TIP!

Try out as many heroes as you can. Some characters will be locked from time to time so it's good not to rely on a single character.

## Developer
**duckarmor**

The creative team behind Q-Clash is duckarmor, led by OrbitalOwen. He has experience in FPS games, having previously created Hex and Combat League.

# ROBLOX CALENDAR

*Roblox is packed with fun 365 days a year. But every now and again a special event will pop up that turns the fun dials to maximum! Take a look at the calendar to get a taste of the cool events that happened last year.*

## LABYRINTH EVENT

The year started with everybody getting lost! The Labyrinth took place in three cool games: Parkour Tag!, Flood Escape 2 and The Labyrinth. Participants who solved the tricky challenges in these games were rewarded with prizes like these:

## EGG HUNT 2018

The year got egg-stremely egg-citing when Egg Hunt 2018: The Great Yolktales was launched! Its brilliant storyline placed you as the saviour in a massive fairytale world. There were 45 eggs to find and collect, each one earning you a cool hat.

## BATTLE ARENA

As summer arrived, Roblox laid down the gauntlet in an all-out fight to the finish with its Battle Arena event. Each battle game included exciting quests that earned players exclusive avatar items.

**JANUARY**

**FEBRUARY**

**MARCH**

**APRIL**

**MAY**

**JUNE**

## 5TH ANNUAL BLOXY AWARDS

One of the biggest events of the year was one of the earliest. The 5th Annual Bloxy Awards honoured the stars of the Roblox community and was watched by millions around the world! The winner of the big prize, Game of the Year, went to Jailbreak by Badimo.

## ATLANTIS EVENT

April is often a wet month, and it was wetter than ever this year when the Atlantis event launched. Players navigated quests in three nautical games – Tradelands, Disaster Island and Sharkbite – to get their hands on aquatic treasures!

## HEROES EVENT

In June, Robloxians got to save the day in the Heroes event. Swordburst 2, Super Hero Life II and Heroes! all put on new challenges for players to conquer. Every quest completed rewarded users with an exclusive avatar item.

## RDC 2018

At the height of summer, the Roblox Developers Conference 2018 kicked off! This event welcomed some of the top developers to San Francisco and Amsterdam, and gave them the chance to learn and collaborate.

## WINTER CREATOR CHALLENGE

Snow way the year was going to go by without the Winter Creator Challenge! Ice cold challenges were completed and frostbitten prizes were won. It was so cool it was sub-zero!

**JULY**

**AUGUST**

**SEPTEMBER**

**OCTOBER**

**NOVEMBER**

**DECEMBER**

## SUMMER TOURNAMENT

The long summer days were filled with fun in the Roblox Summer Tournament! Special challenges were added to Freeze Tag, The Doom Wall II: Burst and Spawn Wars, all of which gave them the chance to win some awesome summer loot.

## HALLOW'S EVE

Things got a bit frightening around the end of October with the Hallow's Eve event! Players needed nerves of steel to beat the bone-chilling quests and challenges. Spooky!

## AQUAMAN WINTER EVENT

The year came to a close with a super heroic event to celebrate the release of Aquaman! Christmas came early for participants, who got their hands on exclusive prizes. What an awesome way to end another amazing year of Roblox!

# COLLABORATIONS

*An essential component of Roblox is its legion of amazing developers. Some choose to work alone, while others prefer to collaborate and create a game-dev supergroup. We're taking a look at some of these amazing partnerships, beginning with the awesome RedManta.*

## REDMANTA

On first glance, you might notice that RedManta release games under their old name, RedMantaStudio, which seems to be a single user. It's actually an account created by co-owners AbstractAlex and Sharksie, under which they release the games they work on together.

### ABSTRACTALEX
AbstractAlex has been a Robloxian since 2009 and has previously released games such as Swordburst Online. His avatar proudly shows off the statuette that the studio won for Robloxian Highschool at the 5th Bloxy Awards!

### SHARKSIE
The other half of RedManta is Sharksie, known almost as well for his avatar's awesome animal-themes. In addition to his work with AbstractAlex, he has also had a hand in other super-successful games like Tiny Tanks!

## QUICKFIRE Q&A

**Q) Why collaborate?**
A) It allows you to focus on core elements of your game while the rest of your team works on other essential features.

**Q) How did you meet?**
A) The Roblox Dev forums, which are full of resources and eager fellow devs.

**Q) Which shortfalls does your collaborator make up for?**
A) They notice bugs that I miss. It's always good to have a second pair of eyes.

**Q) What's your next goal as a collaboration?**
A) Our next goal is to improve the overall social experience of our games.

**– ABSTRACTALEX & SHARKSIE**

# REDMANTA GAMES

What, you may be wondering, can such a star-studded collaboration lead to? Have a peek below to discover a couple of RedManta's gaming gems.

## ROBLOXIAN HIGHSCHOOL

High school has never been so fun! In Robloxian Highschool you can go hang-gliding, buy a super car, breakdance at a club ... or even attend a class or two! You get to customise your avatar to make them look like the coolest kid on campus and make friends with classmates from all over the world.

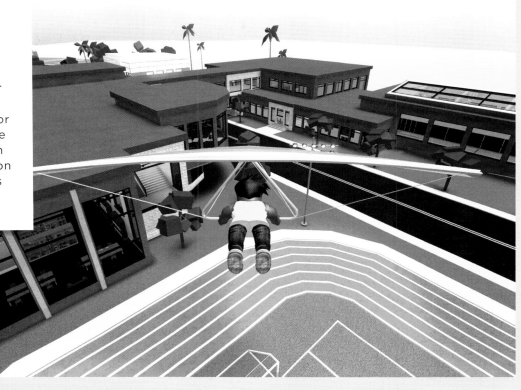

## STORE WARS

Go to war in a store in Store Wars! It really is as simple as it sounds. Two teams sprint around a shop trying to get their hands on any groceries they can weaponise. Use baguettes for close-range battles or lob other items from a distance for ranged combat. The first team to KO the other wins and becomes the supermarket champs!

# ACCELERATORS AND INCUBATORS

*The folks at Roblox HQ are an exceptionally creative bunch, and every year a handful of fortunate developers get the chance to work with them through the Accelerator and Incubator programs. Read on to learn all about the programs and which awesome games they have spawned.*

## ACCELERATED LEARNING

The programs are open to any Roblox developer over the age of 18. They differ very slightly in length and focus – the Accelerator places the onus on improving existing content, while the Incubator tasks you with creating something new – but they have many similarities. If you were to join either program, at the very least you could expect:

✔ The chance to work at Roblox HQ in San Mateo, California

✔ The opportunity to work on your own creation for months and get paid for it

✔ To be able to join as a team and begin to craft a well-oiled game studio

✔ Coaching from Roblox staffers in everything from monetisation to programming AI

✔ To work on industry skills like concept pitches and become familiar with the business side of game development

✔ To push the boundaries of the platform's capabilities and improve it for developers worldwide

✔ A ton of free snacks at HQ

## ACCELERATOR ALUMNI

To join either program is to follow in some very large footsteps. Everyone from Alexnewtron to zKevin has taken part, and some of Roblox's popular games were started, or improved on, within the walls of Roblox HQ.

**LUMBER TYCOON 2**
*Defaultio*

**BOOGA BOOGA**
*Soybeen*

**HEXARIA**
*Biostream/Crykee*

**ROBOT 64**
*zKevin*

# FIRST-HAND EXPERIENCE

So, what's it really like to join one of the programs? We spoke to a couple of devs who are fresh out of the Accelerator program to discover how their experiences went.

## RickyTheFishy
**Fairy World**

"Being a Roblox Accelerator this summer has been a truly wonderful experience that tremendously impacted my career as a developer on the platform. Creating content in an environment full of passionate individuals who share my vision for the platform, as well as the wealth of resources Roblox provided, allowed me to develop my dev and business skills when launching my latest title 'Fairy World'. I intend to apply the knowledge I gathered during my time at Roblox into every endeavour that I take on, as I attempt to grow my game studio. Being an Accelerator has simply been the best experience of my life."

## AlgyLacey
**HACKR**

"The Accelerator program was an amazing experience where I gained a large amount of knowledge about game development in a professional environment. Every day I was able to ask my co-workers in-depth questions and discuss the best way to complete my goals. During the program I worked with two other developers. Previously, we were split around the world and unable to work efficiently due to time-zone differences. However, when we arrived at Roblox we were able to speed up the process and iterate quickly. By the end of the three months we had a working game, which we had already released for beta testing, and a clear plan for the future of the game. For me, the program was a life-changing experience that I will never forget."

# TOP 10 MOST-PLAYED GAMES ON ROBLOX

*The next two in the top 10 couldn't be more different. One's a tricky shoot 'em up and the other is all about finding your fortune deep down underground. The one thing they have in common is a whole lot of fun!*

**8**

## PHANTOM FORCES

If you're on the hunt for an amazing FPS then Phantom Forces is the game you're looking for. Join the Phantoms or the Ghosts and fight for your team around huge maps packed with cool weaponry. You'll need good reflexes and steady nerves as a firefight can break out at any moment and only one team can win!

### READY TO FIGHT!

When you begin, you can select the type of weapons you want to carry from the loadout screen. At first you can only choose from the entry-level guns and melee weapons, but as you progress you will be able to unlock much more powerful variants.

### BASIC TACTICS

It may take a few rounds to get the hang of Phantom Forces – it's fast and furious! Start by getting familiar with the controls and maps. Find teammates and help them when you can. In no time you'll be topping the leaderboard!

### WAYS TO PLAY

There are four modes to play: Flare Domination, where you aim to capture flares around the map; King of the Hill, in which teams battle for control of locations; Kill Confirmed, where extra points are earned for nabbing a fallen enemy's dogtags; and Team Deathmatch, which involves eliminating as many players as possible.

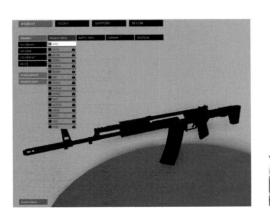

### DEVELOPER
**StyLiS Studios**
*The team behind Phantom Forces includes shaylan007, litozinnamon and AxisAngle.*

# 7

## MINING SIMULATOR

Want to get rich while exploring subterranean worlds? Then Mining Simulator might be the perfect game for you! Grab your pickaxe and dive into the mine to seek your fortune. Will you find gold, silver, or just a big old pile of dirt? You can sell what you find for coins which you can spend on upgrades! You'd better get down there!

The Mine

### TIP!
Talk to the guy near the mine entrance. He'll give you quests to help you understand the game and you'll earn some coins in the process!

### DIG, DIG, DIG!

The only way to improve the basic equipment you start with is to find the mine and dive in. Mine blocks of stone, then sell them for coins back at the surface. You can invest your hard-earned cash in better equipment, which will let you go deeper and find better materials, speeding up your money-making ability.

### PRECIOUS MATERIALS

Most of the stuff you find in the mine is stone, but as you dig deeper, you'll find more valuable things. Fossils and dinosaur bones litter the higher levels of the mine, with copper, quartz, silver and gold further down. Some materials, such as obsidian, can't be mined until you have the right tools.

### MORE MINES!

As you play the game and mine blocks, you'll unlock access to different lands and exotic mines. You can travel to Candy Land, Atlantis, Space and even further afield! Each mine has unique materials to collect and sell.

The Mine

### DEVELOPER
**Rumble Studios**
*This game dev group, led by ObscureEntity, won the Best Studio Bloxy in 2019.*

# ENTER THE EGGVERSE

*Every Easter since 2008, something very special has happened on Roblox – the Egg Hunt! Rediscover the hunts of years past and take a look at some of the most absurdly eggcellent prizes that have been up for grabs in this retrospective.*

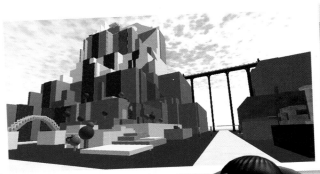

The Egg Hunt has been around almost as long as Roblox, but the first time it had a specially-made game was in 2012. There were 24 eggs hidden around the city and beyond the mountains.

**STAR EGG**
*Vampiric Egg of Twilight*

In 2014 players were asked to Save the Eggverse! The evil Rabid Rabbit stole 34 eggs and scattered them across five maps, each representing a time period from prehistory to the far future.

**STAR EGG**
*Eggy Pop*

**2012**

**2013**

**2014**

**2015**

The number of eggs to find increased for the 2013 hunt. 25 eggs were scattered around a specially-created map with extras to be found on the Roblox website and Studio.

**STAR EGG**
*Egg of Scales*

This time the Egg Hunt was spread across three games: Ripull Minigames, Super Bomb Survival and Twisted Murderer, each of which hosted five exclusive eggs. Six others could be found in all three games.

**STAR EGG**
*Racin' Egg of Fast Cars*

The Egg Hunt was back in 2016 with an Eggcellent Adventure! This egg hunt went back to using one huge map for the first time since 2013. There were 24 eggs to find including the cute tabby egg.

**STAR EGG**
*Tabby Egg*

Egg Hunt 2018: The Great Yolktales featured an evil egg-snatcher: a crow named Aymor! There were 46 eggs to find and to get them all you needed to defeat Aymor. The 2018 entry had the most eggsplosive finale ever!

**STAR EGG**
*Eggplant Egg*

More eggs than ever before had been scattered across nine different locations in Egg Hunt 2017: The Lost Eggs. In total there were 40 eggs to find before players could access a secret area and collect the legendary EBR egg.

**STAR EGG**
*EBR Egg*

# Top 9 Crazy Eggs!

*Yolker Egg, 2018*

*Eggchup, 2018*

*Egg-Bit, 2017*

*Eggtus, 2017*

*Egg Farmer, 2016*

*Luregg, 2014*

*Sorcus Egg, 2013*

*Eggfection, 2018*

*Club Egg Skewer, 2018*

# GAMES YOU MAY HAVE MISSED

*Here we are again with another pair of excellent games that might've evaded your attention. One sends you back in time to the dinosaurs, while the other ships you across the galaxy.*

DINOSAUR SIMULATOR

Take a trip back to a prehistoric era and find out how hard it was to survive in Dinosaur Simulator! You start out as a baby dino and your only aim is survival. Find food, stay healthy and explore your environment, but watch out for deadly predators.

### JURASSIC BLOX
As the game progresses you can explore the vast world and meet the dinosaurs you share it with. Once you've grown up you can start your own prehistoric family!

### DINO FIGHT!
As a baby dino you can't do much but run from trouble. Once you grow up you can fight back and even create a herd with other dinos. Get a big enough herd together and no one will mess with you!

### Developer
**ChickenEngineer**

After creating Dinosaur Simulator, ChickenEngineer continued his animal game journey with DragonVS, a reptilian battle game.

# ECLIPSIS

The planet Eclipsis is rich in iridium, a valuable ore, and it's up to you to secure a steady supply of it for your mysterious corporate employers. Competing companies are also on the hunt, so you'll need to build bases, craft weapons and fend off attacks from other miners!

## BETTER TOGETHER

Blast off from Earth and head to Eclipsis to begin your galactic mining adventure. Collaborate with others to create massive bases complete with shields and artillery.

## WEAPON UP

As you progress you'll find more ways of extracting iridium. You'll also find deadlier weapons to use to fight off attacks or destroy your opponents. The minigun is particularly devastating!

## TIP!

Your most useful gadget is the Portafab. This handy tool extracts iridium and lets you build structures easily. It'll give you a big advantage.

## Developer

### F.F.T.L

Headed up by Davidii, the dev group F.F.T.L (meaning 'Forward, Faster Than Light') also came up with the creative PvP game Build & Battle Redux.

29

# 6TH ANNUAL BLOXY AWARDS

As a new year dawned, Roblox gathered Robloxians from far and wide to celebrate the best of the best on the platform at the 6th Annual Bloxy Awards. Discover some of the winners right here!

## GAME OF THE YEAR

### Bee Swarm Simulator

The Game of the Year went to Bee Swarm Simulator by Onett. It's more impressive as it's the first game Onett has released on Roblox!

## BEST SINGLE-PLAYER GAME

### Escape Room

This puzzling adventure was created by DevUltra. It had previously earned the Bloxy for the Hardest Game at the 5th Annual Awards! Tricky!

## MOBILE GAME OF THE YEAR

### Pet Simulator

For allowing Robloxians to take cute pets everywhere they go, Pet Simulator was awarded the Mobile Game of the Year award.

## BUILDER OF THE YEAR

### TwentyTwoPilots

The innovator behind the Westover Islands series is the recipient of this year's prestigious Builder of the Year award. Not surprising, given that he's created four whole cities for his grand vision.

## STUDIO OF THE YEAR

### Rumble Studios

This game dev group, led by ObscureEntity, is most famous for hits like Mining Simulator, Runway Rumble and Bubble Gum Simulator.

## FAVORITE BREAKOUT GAME

### Destruction Simulator
Winning Favorite *Breakout* Game is very apt for this explosive sim. Players can blow up structures with bombs, rockets and more.

## BEST ART DIRECTION IN A GAME

### Egg Hunt 2018: The Great Yolktales
The latest entry in Roblox's Egg Hunt series took away the award for Best Art for its fairytale-inspired design.

## BUILDERMAN AWARD FOR EXCELLENCE

### Mining Simulator
As if winning Studio of the Year wasn't enough, Rumble Studios also picked up this prestigious trophy for Mining Simulator, released in 2018.

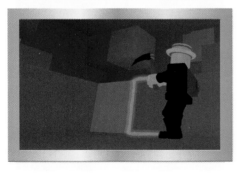

## BEST GUIS

### Phantom Forces
A slick shooter like Phantom Forces has lots of little touches that lift it above the competition, including a clever, understated GUI.

## FAVORITE SHOWCASE

### Neon District
This cyberpunk-themed experience created by InfiniteEffect has welcomed over one million visitors to its brightly lit cityscape.

## MORE AWARDS

**BEST ROUND-BASED GAME**
Flee the Facility

**BEST TUTORIAL**
Welcome to Bloxburg

**QUIRKIEST GAME**
Hmmm

**BEST ROLE PLAYING GAME**
Welcome to Bloxburg

**FAVORITE MAP**
Royale High – The Campus

**BEST LOBBY**
Epic Minigames

**BEST SHOWCASE RENDER**
PumpedRobloxian

**BEST ORIGINAL MUSIC SCORE**
Bslick

**VIDEO OF THE YEAR**
ObliviousHD: The Last Guest

**XBOX GAME OF THE YEAR**
Flood Escape 2

**MOST CONCURRENTS: OVERALL**
MeepCity

**MOST VISITS: OVERALL**
MeepCity

**HIGHEST TOTAL 2018 PLAYTIME**
Jailbreak

**MOST VIP SERVERS SOLD**
Jailbreak

**ROBLOX EVERYDAY AWARD**
Jailbreak

**MOST IMPROVED**
Darkenmoor

**BEST INCUBATOR/ ACCELERATOR GAME**
BOOGA BOOGA

# YOUNITE'S FAVOURITE GAMES

*Roblox builder extraordinaire and wielder of gigantic hammers dropped by to pick his favourite games on the platform. From sneak-em-ups to industrious tycoons, they're all represented.*

*"Every time I visit, I discover something new, and that's what makes me come back to it."*

## STRATOSPHERE SETTLEMENT

Younite chose the atmospheric Stratosphere Settlement by the Elite Builders of Robloxia as his first pick. More an experience than a typical game, it allows you to explore a super-detailed world in the sky. There's loads to discover and marvel at, as well as a handy hub for getting around quickly. Just don't look down!

*"The sheer amount of items and strategies in this custom tycoon are extraordinary."*

## MINER'S HAVEN

Miner's Haven by berezaa Games is the second of Younite's choices. This is a tycoon game like no other. You get to design your base just the way you want, placing droppers, upgraders and furnaces to make as much money as you can! You can also customise your base to your heart's content with cosmetic items from the shop.

"This game requires a lot of quick thinking to ensure you will succeed."

## IN PLAIN SIGHT

Next up is In Plain Sight by all_duck. In this game players are split into a team of thieves and a camera operator. The thieves have to bag as much loot and precious items as they can while the camera operator has to spot them hiding in the crowd and blast them. Dodging the camera is hard work!

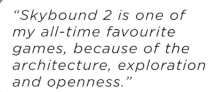

"Skybound 2 is one of my all-time favourite games, because of the architecture, exploration and openness."

## SKYBOUND 2

We're heading upwards for the next pick – Skybound 2 by Imaginaerum. Choose your aircraft, then explore this floating world. Each time you play there are different islands to visit and gems to collect. It's not just about exploring, you also have to fight off any rival pilots you come across.

"A perfect game to play with a bunch of friends."

## KINETIC CODE

Kinetic Code by Team !mpact is Younite's final choice. The game throws you into battle with a team of futuristic soldiers, with one mission – defeat as many opponents as possible. With customisable loadouts and lots of different play styles to try out and master, Kinetic Code is one of the most frantic and strategic FPSs on Roblox.

# HOTTEST ROBLOX TRENDS

*If you've got a few hundred Robux burning a hole in your pocket and have no idea how to spend them, you could make yourself the envy of all Robloxia by splashing out on these Catalog items, which were the most purchased in the last 12 months!*

## BUNDLES

### KORBLOX DEATHSPEAKER

If ever you want to communicate that you're just not in the mood for chatting, slip on the Korblox Deathspeaker outfit. It's a guaranteed deterrent to any overly chatty Robloxians.

### FROST GUARD GENERAL

Chill out, or maybe freeze to the bone, while wearing the Frost Guard General bundle. You'll look cool, that's for certain, but make sure to steer clear of open flames and direct sunlight!

### CIRCUIT BREAKER

Take a break from your fleshy organic form with the Circuit Breaker bundle. It'll make you look like a shiny cyborg and it has the added bonus of being absolutely terrifying! Perfect for scaring your fellow Robloxians.

### SUPERHERO

Forget about going to the gym. Buy the Superhero bundle instead to get a super-powered bod instantly! Even your muscles will have muscles. Use your new paragon persona to save cats from trees.

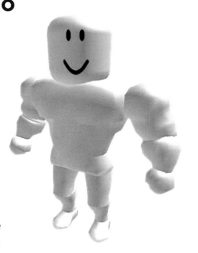

# ACCESSORIES

## BEAR FACE MASK

Hide your feelings behind this ursine mask! Whether you're happy or sad, people will only be able to see a mildly unimpressed bear staring back at them.

## SPARKLING ANGEL WINGS

If you're going to have wings, you may as well make them sparkly and glittery too. That's what you get with this glamorous set.

## CLASSIC SWORDPACK THROWBACK

The Classic Swordpack Throwback oozes a vintage status. Nothing looks more timelessly cool than a pair of razor sharp swords strapped to your back.

## BLACK WINGS

Okay, maybe sparkly wings aren't for all. For those averse to glitter, try these jet black wings instead. You'll still look magical, but with a hidden darkness.

## VIOLET VALKYRIE

Headgear doesn't get more stylish than the Violet Valkyrie. Mix some violet and turquoise, then add in razor-sharp feathers and you've got a fashion hit!

## BLUE TOP HAT

Some classics don't require much explanation. This classic yellow-banded hat is one of them. Wear it when you want to look slightly posh and refined.

## PIRATE CAPTAIN'S HAT

Don this garment and you'll spend more time on the poop deck than you really should, then decide which eye patch goes best with your shoulder parrot.

## GOLDEN SUPER FLY BOOMBOX

Take the hottest jams with you wherever you go with this super-shiny sound system. You can throw an impromptu party anywhere in Robloxia.

# TOP 10 MOST-PLAYED GAMES ON ROBLOX

*The next two games in our top 10 list are all about learning – whether you're hanging out in class or learning how to run a successful restaurant business. Pay attention!*

## 6 ROBLOXIAN HIGHSCHOOL

Robloxian Highschool by RedManta is the school of your dreams. Sure, there are classes like any other school, but there are also skate parks, basketball courts and even an awesome dance club! Will you be a keen student or use school as a place to socialise and have fun?

### COOL SCHOOL!

As a new pupil, it's best to start the game by learning the basics. Take a look at the schedule to find out which class you should be in and head there. Once you're familiar with the layout of the school, you can start checking out the surrounding areas.

### EXTRA-CURRICULAR!

Grab a skateboard and head to the skatepark, play some B-ball on the courts, or go solo and hang-glide around the campus. You're free to do whatever you want!

### CATCH A RIDE

Another neat feature in Robloxian Highschool is the ability to buy cool supercars to race around in. Any of them will make you the talk of the school! When you're tired of racing, head to your dorm and take some time to decorate and get it just how you want it. Then invite your friends over for a dorm party!

### DEVELOPER
**RedManta**
*The team behind Robloxian Highschool also created Super Knife Frenzy and Store Wars.*

# WORK AT A PIZZA PLACE

Some games make it really obvious what they're about. Work At A Pizza Place is one of them! Take on a range of roles and help make Builder Brothers Pizza a success. The biggest challenge is to get a team of people working together to make pizzas ... and money. Here's the lowdown on the work you can take on at BBP.

## COUNTER SERVICE

This role puts you in charge of the front-end customer service. You greet customers with a friendly expression and take their order. When things get busy you might find yourself manning more than one till at a time. Just remember to keep smiling!

## BOXER UPPER

The boxers take the pizzas the chef has made and box them up so they arrive at their destination hot, fresh and, crucially, intact!

## SUPPLY AND DEMAND

The supplier keeps an eye on stock levels. If anything is running low, the suppliers load it into the truck at the supply depot and drop it off at the restaurant.

## OUT FOR DELIVERY

Those pizzas won't deliver themselves! Grab a box, then hop in a car and follow the trail to the customer's door. Once you've dropped a pizza off, race back and repeat!

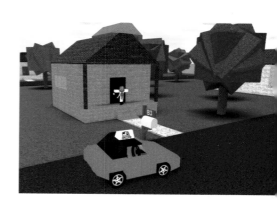

## MASTER CHEF

It wouldn't be a very good pizza place without some hot and tasty food! Check what orders have come in and make the corresponding pizzas. Delicious!

## DEVELOPER
### Dued1

*Work At A Pizza Place was created by Dued1. He's been on Roblox since 2007!*

## HEAD HONCHO

The manager has the sweet perk of being able to hand out bonuses. You can reward the hardest workers or just give a bonus to friends!

# RDC 2018

The Roblox Developer Conference is an invite-only event that gathers members from across the community. Once again, demand was so great that RDC had two separate events. San Francisco and Amsterdam hosted hundreds of Robloxians during two exciting weekends!

## SAN FRANCISCO

The first conference took place in San Francisco and over 400 Robloxians attended. The invited guests had a chance to get to know each other, have fun playing games and learn all about the exciting developments that Roblox has planned for the future. CEO and co-founder David 'Builderman' Baszucki revealed that Roblox is approaching one billion hours of play every month! Some cool upcoming features were shown off, including new lighting effects and physics engines that will shape Roblox games for years to come.

## GAME JAM

One of the most anticipated events at RDC is the Game Jam. This is where teams are given 20 hours to build a game from scratch. The theme for San Francisco's jam was 'alternate physics'.

### BLAST HOOK

The winner of the San Francisco jam was a three player co-operative game where players must take control of one part of a climbing machine and work together to traverse a mountainous obstacle course.

■ Created by nsgriff, Biostream, Quenty, Crykee and Defaultio

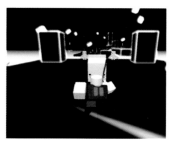

### SPACE JAM

(Runner Up)
This monochromatic parkour game won silver.
■ Created by SnakeWorl, Raguza, Roball1, B_rcode, EchoZenkai and TheBloxDev

### ALTERED SCAPES

(Third Place)
Enter an unusual world of magic and mystery.
■ Created by Mimi_ Dev, Sparklings, BonnabelleRose and DarthChadius

# AMSTERDAM

Amsterdam hosted the European leg of RDC 2018. Over 200 attendees from across the world gathered to celebrate Roblox. The assembled Robloxians had many of the same opportunities as the San Francisco participants, though there was a particular emphasis placed on localisation tools that have been rolled out, so devs can now open their games up to new audiences.

# GAME JAM

The Robloxians of Amsterdam were just as excited about the Game Jam as their American counterparts. The theme this time was 'reflections' and there were some amazing results.

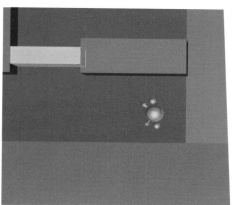

## SPLIT!

The best game in the European jam was a co-op game where you and a friend play as two heroes stuck in different worlds and work together to solve puzzles that impact each others' lands.

■ *Created by Zomebody, Arch_Mage, Ravenshield, Wsly, AlgyLacey, and buildthomas*

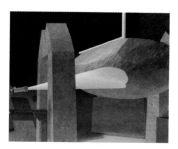

## LIGHTSEEKER

(Runner Up)
Use just a torch to make it through this game.
■ *Created by Basekill, Director1406, Repotted, SteadyOn, jjwood1600 and xXDJducklingXx*

## LUCID DREAM

(Third Place)
Choose your path in this moral adventure.
■ *Created by wind_o, Flubberlutsch, Nawtz and hoshpup*

# GAMES YOU MAY HAVE MISSED

*Here's another pair of games that you may not have played just yet. Make the time to immerse yourself in these experiences and you'll become a parkour pro or legendary baller.*

## FLOOD ESCAPE 2

The water's rising fast, but you've got to move faster to escape it. Created by Crazyblox Games, this successor to the smash hit Flood Escape develops and refines the manic aquatic gameplay and throws even more content into the winning formula.

### BIGGER, BETTER, FASTER

The maps in Flood Escape 2 come in four difficulties, ranging from the simple Easy to the brutally challenging Insane mode! You tackle each map with a group of up to 11 other players and work together to activate buttons, which will get rid of obstacles and let you proceed to the next part of the map.

### WATERWORLD

As in the original, the aim is to parkour your way through mazy maps, running and jumping to avoid the rising water.

## Developer

**Crazyblox Games**

Developer Crazyblox also created the first game in the series, Flood Escape, and has been on the Roblox platform since 2008.

# RB WORLD 2

Get on the court and live out your hoop dreams. RB World 2 is a sports simulation created by ace developer CollegiateJokes. The game starts in the locker room, where you design your fledgling basketball legend, before hitting the court to shoot some hoops.

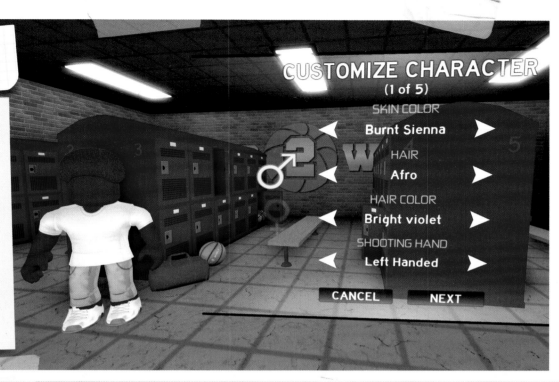

## SLAM DUNK!

Take a trip to your gym first, where you can practise your shooting and jumping. Your gym is fully customisable, so as soon as you start earning some Koins you can adapt it just the way you want it. When you're ready to compete, head outside and pick a court to play on!

## THREE-POINTER

It's best to start out playing 2v2 games in the park and work your way up to the Rec Centre. On your way you'll meet players to team up with and improve your game. It's not just about going for the hoop. Support your teammates by passing and helping out defensively and you'll go a long way.

## TIP!

Get a group together and you can create your own League. Host tournaments and cement your reputation as the RB World 2 champion!

## Developer
### CollegiateJokes

CollegiateJokes has been a Robloxian since 2009 and started his dev career with the prequel, RB World.

# ROBLOX CREATOR CHALLENGE – PART 2

*It's time to continue along the path to game dev mastery. You already have a beginning and end point, but now it's time to design the level in between. Read on to find out how to create your tricky obby course and learn about the importance of playtesting.*

**10** In the menu bar, look for a button called 'Part'. Press the little arrow underneath it to choose a shape to add in your world. Choose the Cylinder option to add it to the workspace as 'Part'. Rename it 'Pillar'.

**11** Select 'Pillar' in the Explorer and you will see a list of properties in the Properties tab. You can experiment with properties like BrickColor and Material to change the look. Just change the pillar colour for now.

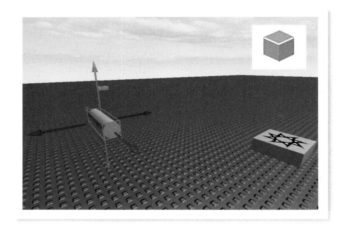

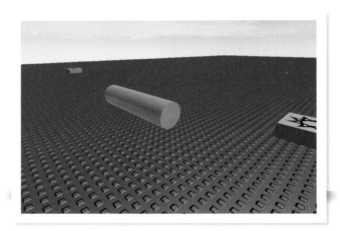

**12** Use the scale and rotate options to turn it into a large vertical pillar. Now move it closer to SpawnPoint1, then drop the SpawnPoint on top of it. Right-click the Pillar to duplicate it, then move it beneath SpawnPoint2, before moving SpawnPoint2 to the top.

**13** Create more parts of different shapes and sizes to create a tricky obby route between the two Pillars. If you want a part to float in the air, you'll need to anchor it, meaning the physics engine won't make it fall. You can do this by selecting the part and pressing the Anchored icon in the toolbar, or by checking the Anchored box in Properties.

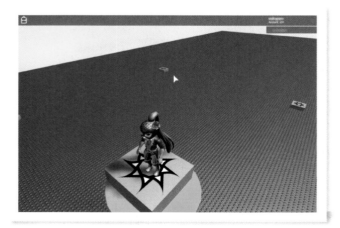

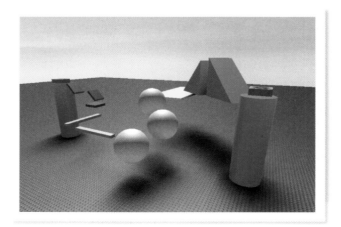

**14** Now we'll create the second part of the route using the Terrain tool. Press the Editor button and you'll see the Terrain Editor window appear. From here you'll have access to eight tools to use.

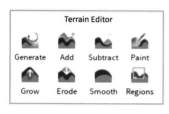

**15** Select 'Add' from the menu and add some terrain beneath SpawnPoint3. Your SpawnPoint will be buried under a mound, but don't worry for now. Select 'Grow' from the Terrain Editor and click on the mound to make it as tall as the pillars you made. Select SpawnPoint3 in the Explorer and move it to the top of the mound.

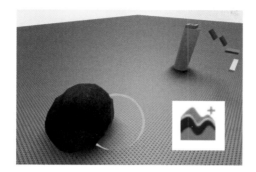

**16** Now create the route between a Pillar and the mound by creating new terrains or adding to the one you just made. Terrain must be added to an item already in the world, like the baseplate, but you can use the 'Subtract' tool to remove areas touching the floor so they float. Terrain is anchored by default.

**17** When you select a tool in Terrain Editor, your cursor will turn into a brush, and you'll see a number of Brush Options you can change, including brush size, strength and shape. You can also choose the material you're using to make terrain. Play with these settings to give the route more interest.

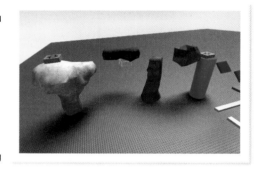

**18** Finally, create two more routes to make a full circuit between all four SpawnPoints. The routes don't have to be straight lines. Make them with a mixture of terrain and parts, and leave some larger platforms so we can add in extra objects in the next section.

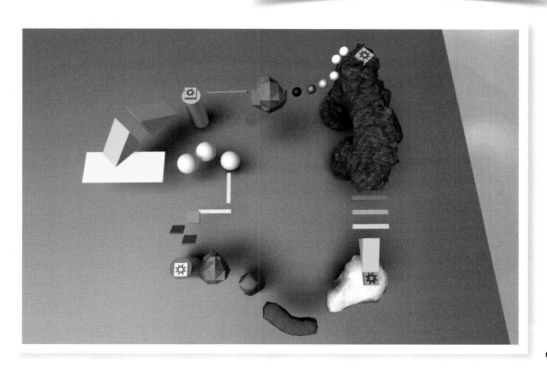

# PETEYK473'S FAVOURITE GAMES

*This multi-talented Robloxian has helped to build many games and also manages the Roblox Localization Team, which helps to translate games. Here are his five fave games on the platform.*

> "Scavenging the lands looking for rare and interesting creatures and materials is so interesting!"

## FANTASTIC FRONTIER

PeteyK473's first pick is the awesome Fantastic Frontier by Spectrabox. This expansive adventure game lets you roam the wild and dangerous fantasy land to make your fortune. Hunt, fish, mine, or just pick mushrooms, battling mythical creatures along the way. The further you explore, the more rewards you'll receive.

> "The game is best played with a group of friends – the more the better."

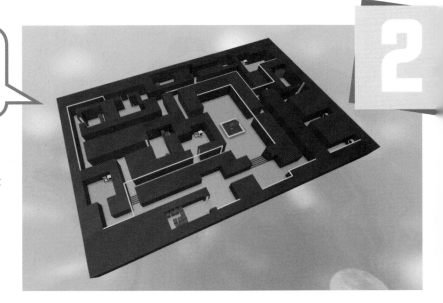

## DECEPTION INFECTION

Next up is Deception Infection by Stickmasterluke. One player is infected, but no one knows who. The infected player has to deceive others and get close to infect them, all while the map slowly floods, pushing players closer together. It's a race to solve the mystery before drowning!

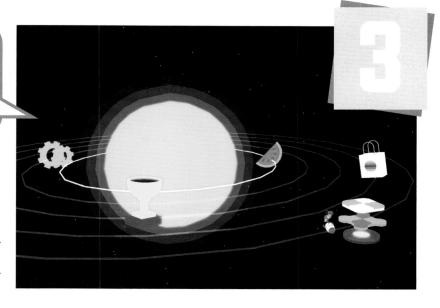

## ROLLERNAUTS

Smash, blast and roll your way to victory in Rollernauts by Numoji. Controlling a little astronaut balancing on top of a ball, each game takes place on a floating island and tasks you with knocking others off the edge. Scattered around are power-ups that can give you a big advantage over other players.

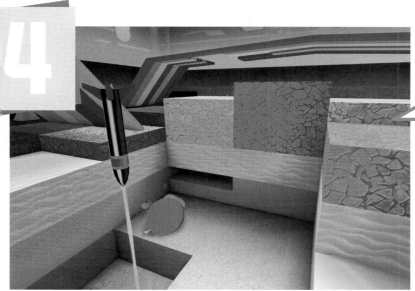

## SUPER BOMB SURVIVAL

Grab your umbrella! It's raining bombs in Super Bomb Survival by Polyhex. Players run around a tightly packed arena, dodging bombs falling from the sky. Each bomb destroys a bit of the arena, so as a round goes on the arena gets smaller, making it harder to avoid subsequent barrages.

## SUPER BLOCKY BALL

PeteyK473's final pick is madcap racer Super Blocky Ball by Maelstronomer. You're encased in a giant see-through ball and must roll your way along hazard-filled courses to beat your competitors and win the race. This game is best played with loads of competitive buddies!

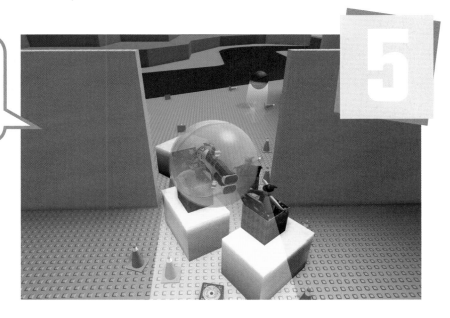

# COLLABORATIONS

*It's entirely possible to make a game by yourself on Roblox, but sometimes two heads can be better than one. We're taking a close look at teams on the platform and the second game dev group under our microscope is Block Evolution Studios.*

## BLOCK EVOLUTION STUDIOS

Consisting of the similarly named BlockFaceSteve and Blockfacebob, Block Evolution Studios has only been active since 2017. However, in the few years that have passed, they've already released five mega-successful games, including Vet Simulator, Heists and Build with Friends.

### BLOCKFACEBOB
This dinosaur fan – just check out that avatar – has been on Roblox for over a decade. He'd previously released a game on his own, Zombie Defence Tycoon, which has been played over 300,000 times!

### BLOCKFACESTEVE
The other half of Block Evolution Studios is BlockFaceSteve, who joined the platform in 2010. As well as being the co-founder of a successful studio, he also earned a Paintball MVP trophy in 2011.

## QUICKFIRE Q&A

**Q) Why collaborate?**
A) Collaboration for us benefits development and productivity in loads of ways. We can bounce ideas off each other, solve each other's problems, keep one another motivated and share our knowledge.

**Q) How did you meet?**
A) We met at university while working on a couple of Robotics projects. We decided to produce Zoo Tycoon under the group Block Evolution Studios.

**Q) What is your collaboration's next goal?**
A) We recently developed a game in only 3 days and we're working on adding content to it. Over the next few months we plan to update existing games and maybe develop a big project later!

**– BLOCKFACESTEVE**

# BLOCK EVOLUTION STUDIOS GAMES

## ZOO TYCOON

Start your own animal haven and make it a huge success in Zoo Tycoon. You'll need to start by opening tills and building enclosures, then you can fill them with exotic animals. Smaller ones like tortoises can be picked up, while big ones will need more enticing. The more animals you've got, the more money you'll rake in!

## JURASSIC TYCOON

If Zoo Tycoon isn't dangerous enough, try Jurassic Tycoon! The principle is similar, but in this game the chances of being eaten alive are much higher. Grab your tranq guns and go catch some dinos! You can land loads of prehistoric beasts, including the deadly T. rex and the spiky Stegosaurus!

## HEISTS

Heists puts you in control of a crafty criminal with a cool hideout. Your mission is to fill your vault with as much loot as possible and stop anyone from taking it. Players will try to break into your base, but don't worry, you can break into their hideouts and steal goodies from them too!

# TOP 10 MOST-PLAYED GAMES ON ROBLOX

We're getting close to the top slot in our countdown of the most-played games on Roblox, but before we get there we have numbers 3 and 4 to check out. They're a pair of games that are perfect for playing socially!

## ROYALE HIGH

Royale High is a school like no other! Fancy cars and dream dorm rooms – this place is all about luxury living. Go to class and work hard to gain XP and level up. Ride around campus in a cool car, then take part in the Royale High Dance. Maybe you'll be voted dance king or queen!

### LOVE TO LEARN

It's really important to show up to all your classes on time and work hard. The harder you work, the better the grade you'll get and the faster you'll level up. Take classes in art, chemistry, baking, computers, music and more! You'll be a mega-brain after doing all of those!

### ROBLOXIAN'S BEST FRIEND

Diamonds are the shiny currency at Royale High. Find them around the campus or earn them by levelling up. You can spend diamonds on customisation, having food at the café, or buying lush new furniture for your dorm.

### CUSTOMISE

A cool feature of Royale High is being able to control the appearance of your avatar. Earn diamonds and spend them on hairstyles, outfits, wings and so much more. You can change the colour of items and combine them for added effect. Top your outfit off with a swish crown for the ultimate Royale High look.

### DEVELOPER

**callmehbob**

*callmehbob is the developer behind Royale High. She's been on Roblox since 2007.*

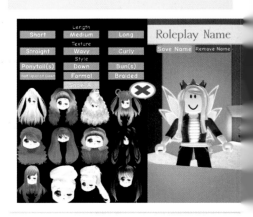

# WELCOME TO BLOXBURG

Travel to the city and make a success of yourself in Welcome to Bloxburg by Coeptus. The city is packed full of opportunities and ways to play. Start off by buying a small plot of land and use it to build your dream house, then get a job to earn money and spend it all buying cool stuff and having fun!

## NO PLACE LIKE HOME

One of the best features in Welcome to Bloxburg is being able to build your own home. Players in a hurry can use one of the nifty house templates. If you want to take a bit more time, you can go wild designing and building a dream home. Choose everything from the colour of the front door to the type of sink in the bathroom!

## WORK IT!

Bloxburg has many career opportunities. Try your hand at being a hairdresser, woodcutter, delivery person, ice cream seller, mechanic, janitor, pizza chef and more! Some jobs are harder than others and some pay more. Earn more money by levelling up and being excellent at your chosen job.

## CITY LIFE

Bloxburg is an interesting place to explore. Start by climbing the mountain and hopping on the hang-glider to get your bearings. Visit the club to try out your dancing skills, then get some rest on the beach. You can even enjoy a holiday at the campsite or stargaze at the city observatory!

## DEVELOPER
### Coeptus
*Don't be fooled by his humble look. This is the Bloxy-winning dev behind Welcome to Bloxburg!*

# NEXT GEN AVATARS

*When you think of Roblox, you may think of the blocky avatars that populate Robloxia, but they're starting to evolve. Roblox released the Rthro avatars, which offer increased customisation options, more realistic proportions and better animations. Let's take a look at them!*

## WHAT IS RTHRO?

The Rthro avatar is the latest variation of the beloved avatar. It allows players to modify the proportions of their character, from the slightly skewed scale of the R15 to a true representation of the human form.

R6

R15

RTHRO

## INCREASED CUSTOMISATION

So how do you make your avatar into an Rthro variant? Go to the Avatar Editor, select the Body tab, then Scale. You'll see two new options – Body Type and Proportions. Move both scales as far to the right as you can and there you have it – your very own Rthro-ready avatar.

## RTHRO SHOWCASE

While you can scale any outfit to new Rthro proportions, Roblox has also released a number of awesome costumes specifically designed to work with the new scales. These can be worn like any other outfit.

# RTHRO IN ACTION

Now that your avatar is fully Rthro, it's time to take it out for a spin. Drop into any of the below Rthro-supporting games to admire the new avatar animations ... and to show off your new avatar, of course.

EPIC MINING

WORK AT A COFFEE SHOP

HEISTS

SUPER BOMB SURVIVAL

# COLLABORATIONS

It's time for a look at one last incredible Roblox collaboration and this time it's a trio of awesome devs. StyLiS Studios are the collective brains behind one of Roblox's biggest and most technically impressive games, Phantom Forces!

## STYLIS STUDIOS

The seeds of StyLiS Studios were planted years ago, when a young litozinnamon and shaylan007 were playing games together on Roblox. Fast-forward to present day and you have a game dev group that lives on the cutting edge of what is possible on the platform.

### LITOZINNAMON
The first of the StyLiS Studios team, litozinnamon has been a Robloxian since 2009. Before setting up StyLiS studios, he previously worked on smash-hit shooter Call of Robloxia 5.

### SHAYLAN007
Super-green dev shaylan007 is the next member of StyLiS Studios. He is the master modeller behind the majority of the game you see, including the multitude of weapons.

### AXISANGLE
AxisAngle, the smartly-dressed math-whiz of the group, used his tech skills to perfect the physics-heavy gameplay of Phantom Forces. He first joined the platform over a decade ago!

## QUICKFIRE Q&A

**Q) Why collaborate?**
A) Because it would take too long to make a game like Phantom Forces as a solo developer.

**Q) How did you meet?**
A) litozinnamon and shaylan007 met way back in the early 2010s as online friends playing Roblox games together. AxisAngle completed the trio when they started making Phantom Forces.

**Q) What shortfalls of yours do your collaborators make up for?**
A) In our team, shaylan007 covers essentially all aspects of modelling, while AxisAngle's mathematical knowledge and experience covers a lot of programming.

**Q) What is your collaboration's next goal?**
A) With the introduction of Roblox on consoles, we hope to optimise Phantom Forces to be playable on this lucrative platform, while keeping up-to-date with the PC version at all times.

– LITOZINNAMON

# STYLIS STUDIOS GAMES

Sometimes a studio's output is more about quality than quantity. That is most definitely the case for StyLiS, who have, so far, only released one game. However, that game has won several Bloxy Awards, been played over half a billion times, and received constant updates since its creation in 2015.

## PHANTOM FORCES

Phantom Forces is a team-based multiplayer shooter. It's packed full of amazing physics meaning that the combat is more realistic than many games you've played on Roblox. Phantom Forces drops you into one of two teams and gives you an objective to complete your mission before your enemies can complete theirs, using an arsenal of realistic weapons.

# 6TH ANNUAL BLOXY AWARDS

*For the first time ever, Roblox had an Innovation category that recognised the contributions of multiple Robloxians per award. Here's the complete list of winners for each one, as well as the Roblox Community Creators awards.*

## GAMEPLAY

### Book of Monsters, Pet Simulator, Bee Swarm Simulator, Q-Clash

With so many new advancements occuring on Roblox, one could almost be forgiven for forgetting about core gameplay – not these four games, which were rewarded for excelling in that department.

BOOK OF MONSTERS

## RTHRO

### Heists, Broken Bones

For their support of the emerging Rthro avatars, Heists by Block Evolution Studios and Broken Bones by Zaquille received this award.

BROKEN BONES

## BEST SCRIPTERS

### Crazyman32, ObscureEntity, NewFissy, LordJurrd, Mightybaseplate, ScriptOn, Buildthomas

The award for the best coders of the year went to an assortment of devs that have created innovative games, including LordJurrd for Island Royale, NewFissy for VentureLand and ObscureEntity for his work on Mining Simulator.

NEWFISSY          CRAZYMAN32

## LOCALIZATION

### MeepCity, Adopt Me, Welcome to Bloxburg, Deathrun, Theme Park Tycoon

2018 was the year that localization was brought to the forefront of Roblox, and five games were given this award to recognise their endeavours to make their games more international.

DEATHRUN

## ROBLOX COMMUNITY CONTRIBUTOR

### Crazyman32, Ysko AlvinBlox, zKevin

We all know that Roblox is a friendly place to hang out, but there are some Robloxians who go above and beyond, like these Roblox heroes who received a Bloxy for outstanding community contribution.

ZKEVIN

## TECHNICAL ACHIEVEMENTS

### Vesteria, Hostile Skies, Strucid Alpha

For pushing the technological limits of the platform, three games received this prestigious Bloxy award.

## MORE AWARDS

**BEST VIDEO CHANNEL**
InquisitorMaster

**BEST COMEDIC VIDEO**
ItsFunneh: Getting Buff

**BEST ACTION VIDEO**
ObliviousHD: The Last Guest 3

**BEST MUSIC VIDEO**
KawaiiUnicorn: Don't Call Me A Noob

**BEST FAN ART**
RBLXcrackop

**BEST GIF**
supernob12three

**FAVORITE LIVE STREAMER**
ThinkNoodles

**BEST GAME TRAILER**
Mining Simulator

**BEST TWEET**
Badimo

**BEST SOCIAL GROUP**
Bee Swarm Simulator Group

**BEST TWITTER CHANNEL**
KreekCraft

HOSTILE SKIES

**55**

# WOOT3'S FAVOURITE GAMES

The last of our Robloxian-chosen favourites comes from Roblox intern and founder of Fracture Studios, Woot3! What are his favourite games? Read on to find out.

**1**

"After a lot of practice, I am actually starting to get good at it, trying new songs that I was never able to beat before!"

## ROBEATS

Woot3's first pick is rhythm game RoBeats. Developed by RobeatsDev, this game lets you take part in 4-player rhythm battles! There's an eclectic selection of songs to jam along to, and you unlock more as you play. If you don't fancy playing you can hop into spectator mode and watch the action.

"This game is a brilliant example of one that is easy to play but difficult to master."

**2**

## HEX

Fast-paced shooter Hex, created by OrbitalOwen, is Woot3's next pick. It features massive maps to battle on as well as tons of cool weapons and awesome customisables to unlock. Hex has been around since 2014, but it's still tons of fun!

"Every time you join there's a new experience – perhaps you'll rob the Bank today or how about the Jewelry Store?"

## JAILBREAK

Cops or robbers? You get to choose a role in Woot3's next game, Jailbreak, developed by super duo Badimo! Pick a side and then get to work stopping crime or committing it! Prisoners start off in jail and have to break out before they can resume their criminal careers. Guards have to stop prisoners escaping and foil any crimes they commit.

"It combines the thrill of a classic arcade racer with all the fun of a marble run."

## SUPER BLOCKY BALL

Be the quickest out of the blocks and first on the leaderboard in Super Blocky Ball by Maelstronomer. You control a giant ball and race against other players through twisting tracks that have multiple routes and shortcuts. There are plenty of obstacles getting in your way, so you'll need speed and skill to win!

"Having grown up by an amusement park it's not surprising I've spent longer playing this than any game!"

## THEME PARK TYCOON 2

Ever wanted to build a rollercoaster? Of course you have, and you get to do that and much more in Theme Park Tycoon 2 by Den_S. Starting with a small plot of land, you'll soon have rides, stalls and amusements. You can reinvest earnings in bigger, better and faster rides! By the end you'll have the theme park of your dreams!

# ROBLOX CREATOR CHALLENGE – PART 3

*Your obby is in place and easy to navigate, but where's the challenge? In this final section, we're going to look at how to add a little peril to your game with some life-sapping hazards. Don't worry, we'll also add a few powerups to help you too!*

**19** To create your first hazard, we're simply going to find the Baseplate in the Explorer and … delete it. Not only does this create an abyss to fall into, but it also gives you the opportunity to give your course a full run-through. Hit Play, make sure you're able to overcome all obstacles, and that when you fall you respawn at the point you were supposed to spawn.

**20** Now we'll create a hazard that drains health when you touch it. Create a small, red Part, so you can place it repeatedly and it instantly warns the player of danger. Now to hammer home the message, we'll add an effect. With the Part selected in the Explorer, click the Model option from the menu bar and then select the Effects button. Choose the Fire effect to make the part look even more dangerous.

**21** Next, it's finally time to get scripting! Right-click on your hazard Part, press Insert Object and choose 'Script'. This will open the scripting window, which should just have a generic 'Hello World' print statement. Delete the statement and copy in the text below in its place.

| | |
|---|---|
| Sets how often damage can be triggered | Controls how much damage the part does |
| | Gets a reference to the Part the script is attached to |

A method that is called when the Part the script is attached to is touched

```
local DAMAGE = 5
local COOLDOWN = 2

local parentPart = script.Parent

local recentlyDamagedCharacters = {}

local function onTouch(otherPart)

    local character = otherPart.Parent
    local humanoid = character:FindFirstChildWhichIsA("Humanoid")
    local player = game:GetService("Players"):GetPlayerFromCharacter(character)

    if player and humanoid and not recentlyDamagedCharacters[character] then
        humanoid:TakeDamage(DAMAGE)
        recentlyDamagedCharacters[character] = true
        wait(COOLDOWN_IN_SECONDS)
        recentlyDamagedCharacters[character] = nil
    end
end

parentPart.Touched:Connect(onTouch)
```

Stores the players who have recently been damaged by the trap

Checks whether the character is a player and has not been recently damaged

Waits for the cooldown to time out before continuing

Finds the character that is touching the part, stores whether it is a humanoid and finds the player in the game.

Damages the player and adds it to the table of recently damaged characters

Removes the player from the table of recently damaged characters

Connects the event 'Touched' to the 'onTouch' function above

**22** Run your game and you should take damage when you touch the hazard. To make the course more challenging, duplicate the hazard multiple times and place them around your course. Make sure they're not completely unavoidable because that wouldn't be fair. Test and re-test until you're happy. You can change the parts as you duplicate them to make varied hazards too.

**23** Time to add some healing powers. With one small change to the script, you can create the ability to heal. You could make a healing Part, but we're going to add a script to the SpawnPoints, so you can heal after a tricky section. Click the SpawnPoint, click Insert Object, then choose Script. Copy the code from your hazard script to your new one. Then make this single change to the script you copied:

```
local DAMAGE = -100
```

If a positive value like DAMAGE = 5 subtracts five health points, then adding a minus number like -100 becomes a positive and results in healing! This will heal the player fully. Copy the script and apply it to all of the SpawnPoints.

**24** And there you have it – a simple obby game, built from different parts and terrain, with hazards that damage your health and checkpoints that heal you and record your progress. Not bad – you're on your way to becoming a fully-fledged game dev. But this is just a starting point. Here are a few ideas on how you can expand this game:

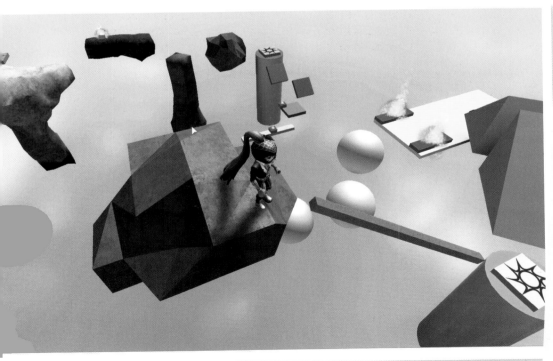

▓ Make the obby longer. Add increasingly longer sections to your level, with more hazards, jumps and checkpoints.

▓ Use the Toolbox – it has loads of items built by the community. Why not make a frozen level with penguins and igloos, or a junkyard full of different vehicles?

▓ Let other people play – see which bits they found too hard or too easy and change the level based on their feedback.

▓ Visit developer.roblox. com/learn-roblox/all-tutorials to find out more about the different things you can add to your game. There are dozens of articles that will be able to help you.

▓ Most importantly, have fun!

# ROBLOX SWAG

*You've customised and styled your avatar to perfection, but what about you? Don't worry! Roblox has plenty of swag in the real world too! Check out some of the coolest items available.*

## TEES!

As well as being a perfectly practical piece of clothing, the Roblox tee range is totally awesome.

Builderman and his pals are here to remind you to Build Greater!

The classic Roblox logo on a funky two-tone split tee.

This awesome black tee looks like it's crumbling away into blox!

Fading aquatic blue t-shirt with a crumbling Roblox logo. Nice!

This long-sleeved top is the perfect way to show off some cool characters.

Mr. Robot encourages the wearer of this tee to be more like him.

## HATS!

Stay warm in the winter and/or cool in the summer.

A knitted black beanie with a red and white logo design. Keeps your head toasty.

Red flat-bill cap with a character pattern, perfect for summer days.

## BOOKS!

The Roblox library is expanding – in addition to this awesome Annual, there's a sticker book and a game guide to grow your collection!

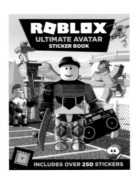

### ULTIMATE AVATAR STICKER BOOK

Use hundreds of stickers straight from the Catalog to create the ultimate avatar for a dozen different game scenarios. Let your imagination run wild!

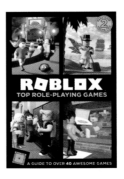

### ROBLOX TOP ROLE-PLAYING GAMES

Discover over 40 games from the role-playing genre in this handy game guide, featuring everything from Book of Monsters to Vehicle Simulator.

# TOYS!

The wide world of Roblox and all the characters in it means there are endless toys to collect. Each one comes with an exclusive virtual item too! Take a look at some of the newest and most awesome!

## CORE FIGURES
Iconic characters packaged in a set with accessories.

## 6-PACK
Six different figures in an overstuffed pack. Perfect for playing or displaying.

## GAME PACK
A small playset with characters and items from a single game.

## MIX & MATCH SET
Characters with interchangeable parts so you can customise to your heart's content.

## PLAYSETS
These huge sets have everything you need to recreate your favourite games, with dozens of accessories.

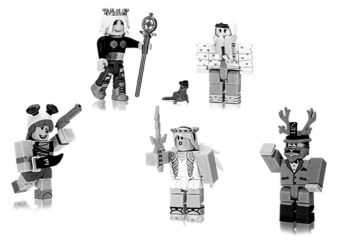

## VEHICLES
Get your Roblox figures on the move with these vehicle collections from popular games.

## MYSTERY FIGURES
Each mystery box contains a character figure and an accessory. As you might have guessed, it's a complete mystery which one you'll get!

# TOP 10 MOST-PLAYED GAMES ON ROBLOX

*Here they are, the two most-played games on Roblox – and for the second year in a row too! Whether you want to take part in a crime caper, or just hang out with friends, these games have you covered!*

## 2 MEEPCITY

Take a trip to MeepCity to hang with friends, play games, build a house and adopt a meep! MeepCity was developed by Alexnewtron and was the first game to get a billion visits! That's a lot of Robloxians taking the trip to the city to socialise and have fun!

### MEEP LIFE

Meeps are a big part of MeepCity life. These cute creatures are available at the pet shop. Once you get one, you can change its colour and name it, or invest in some cool headgear. When you've built your own house, you'll even be able to fill it with meep furniture to make the little guy feel at home.

### GONE FISHING

You can earn money by heading to the lake to go fishing! The fishing minigame is a test of skill and patience. Any fish you catch can be taken to the pet shop and exchanged for coins.

### STARBALL

Take your meep along for a game of Starball! In this minigame your meep rolls around courses in a giant ball. You must guide your meep through each puzzle, grabbing stars to earn coins. There are four levels to complete, including Candy Land and Sunny Fields.

### DEVELOPER
**Alexnewtron**
*Alexnewtron is the mayor of MeepCity, and has won many Bloxy Awards for his social game.*

# JAILBREAK

Hitting the number one spot in our countdown is none other than Jailbreak! This escape sim lets you choose between the police and prisoner teams. You're either upholding the law of the land or breaking it. It's fun to switch between the two and use what you've learned to get better at escaping or catching people!

## ESCAPE!

Playing as a prisoner means you start off locked up in jail. To make progress, you need to find a way out of the facility. There are a few ways of doing this: escape through the sewer, blow up a wall, or steal a keycard from an officer and just walk out through the door! The choices are many, but all result in freedom!

## CRIME WAVE

When you leave the prison you'll be on the wanted list, so move fast. Any guard you come across will be able to arrest you. Once you've escaped, you can start committing crimes. Rob the bank, steal jewels, do whatever you can before you're thrown back in jail!

## THE BLUE LINE

Choosing to play as the police means it's up to you to hunt down the escaped criminals. You have a pair of handcuffs that will clip on to crooks you get close to, plus any car you get in turns into a police car, complete with flashing lights. Keep an eye out for any crimes in progress and head in that direction quickly!

## DEVELOPER

**Badimo**
*Duo asimo3089 and badcc won Studio of the Year at the 5th Annual Bloxy Awards!*

# RECAP QUIZ

We're almost at the end of our journey, but first, let's see how much you were paying attention. The answers to all questions are somewhere in this book. Read through again if you don't know the answers.

## EASY

Let's get started with some simple questions. You might have already known the answers to these before you read the book.

**Which was the top most-played game of the past 12 months?**

☐ MeepCity ☐ Jailbreak ☐ Bee Swarm Simulator

**What is the name of the latest avatar evolution?**

☐ R15 ☐ Rhuman ☐ Rthro

**Which game did StyLiS Studios create?**

☐ Tiny Tanks ☐ Phantom Forces ☐ Polyguns

**Which of these is not a program that Roblox runs for developers?**

☐ Incubator ☐ Instigator ☐ Accelerator

**Who won Builder of the Year at the 6th Annual Bloxy Awards?**

☐ ElevenDrivers ☐ TwentyTwoPilots ☐ ThirtyThreeSailors

**Which of these was one of the most popular Catalog packages this year?**

☐ Circuit Breaker ☐ Circuit Builder ☐ Circuit Transformer

**Which tricky event occurred in January 2018?**

☐ Labyrinth ☐ Heroes ☐ Battle Arena

*Starting to get a little harder now. You'll definitely need to have had a good read-through to get these right.*

**Which European city was RDC 2018 held in?**

☐ Berlin          ☐ Brussels          ☐ Amsterdam

**Which of these is not a Terrain Tool in Roblox Studio?**

☐ Add          ☐ Subtract          ☐ Divide

**Which of these is not a member of Block Evolution Studios?**

☐ BlockFaceSteve          ☐ Blockfacebob          ☐ BlockfaceJeff

**Who developed RB World 2?**

☐ ScriptOn          ☐ CollegiateJokes          ☐ Dued1

# HARD

*Are these trick questions? Nope, but they are pretty difficult. Make sure you read every page thoroughly!*

**What was the subtitle of 2017's Egg Hunt?**

☐ The Lost Eggs          ☐ Egg Battle          ☐ Eggsplosive Adventure

**Where can you get ready-made models in Roblox Studio?**

☐ Properties          ☐ Effects          ☐ Toolbox

**Which of these games did not host the Atlantis event in April?**

☐ Tradelands          ☐ Sharkbite          ☐ Booga Booga

**Who manages the Roblox Localization team?**

☐ PeteyK473          ☐ PixelatedCandy          ☐ DarthChadius

# SEE YOU ON ROBLOX!

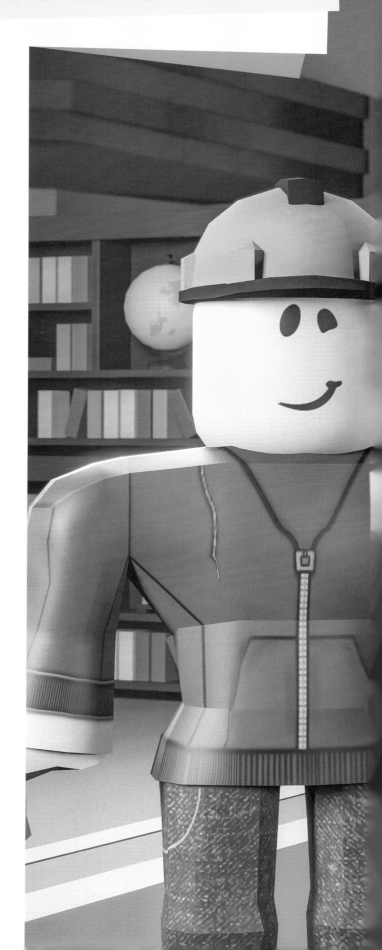

**Thank you so much for accompanying me on this journey to discover all the amazing stories and experiences our community has brought to life over the past year.**

Looking toward the future, I see an enormous opportunity ahead of us. Millions of people are coming to Roblox not just to play games, but to share and interact. We're building a place where people around the world can go fishing together, work at a restaurant together, survive a tornado together, or participate in a fashion show with friends. We are bringing the world together through play.

I've been humbled by the love and support from the community, and I can't thank you enough for being a fan. Your imagination never ceases to inspire and amaze me.

It's been fun! I look forward to seeing you on Roblox soon.

Sincerely,
**David Baszucki, a.k.a. Builderman**

# A GUIDE TO SOCIALISING ONLINE WITH ROBLOX

## YOUNGER FANS' GUIDE TO ROBLOX

Spending time online is great fun! Roblox might be your first experience of digital socialising, so here are a few simple rules to help you stay safe and keep the internet a great place to spend time.

■ *Never give out your real name – don't use it as your username.*

■ *Never give out any of your personal details.*
■ *Never tell anybody which school you go to or how old you are.*
■ *Never tell anybody your password except a parent or guardian.*
■ *Always tell a parent or guardian if something is worrying you.*

## PARENTS' GUIDE TO ROBLOX

*Roblox has security and privacy settings that enable you to monitor and limit your child's access to the social features on Roblox, or turn them off completely. You can also limit the range of games your child can access, view their activity histories and report inappropriate activity on the site. Instructions for how to use these safety features are listed below.*

## NAVIGATING ROBLOX'S SAFETY FEATURES

*To restrict your child from playing, chatting and messaging with others on Roblox, log into your child's account and click on the **gear icon** in the upper right-hand corner of the site and select **Settings**. From here you can access the **Security** and **Privacy** menus:*

■ *Users register for Roblox with their date of birth. It's important for children to enter the correct date because Roblox has default security and privacy settings that vary based on a player's age. This can be checked and changed in **Settings**.*

■ *To review and restrict your child's social settings, go to **Settings** and select **Privacy**. Review the options under **Contact Settings** and **Other Settings**. Select **No one** or **Everyone**. Note: players age 13 and older have additional options.*

■ *To control the safety features that are implemented on your child's account, you'll need to set up a 4-digit PIN. This will lock all of the settings, only enabling changes once the PIN is entered. To enable an Account PIN, go to the **Settings** page, select **Security** and turn **Account PIN** to **ON**.*

*To help monitor your child's account, you can view the history for certain activities:*

■ *To view your child's private message history, choose **Messages** from the menu bar down the left-hand side of the main screen. If the menu bar isn't visible, click on the **LIST** icon in the left-hand corner.*

■ *To view your child's chat history with other players, open the **Chat & Party** window, located in the bottom-right of the page. Once this window is opened, you can click on any of the listed users to open a window with the chat history for that particular account.*

■ *To view your child's online friends and followers, choose **Friends** from the menu bar down the left-hand side of the main screen.*

■ *To view your child's creations, such as games, items, trades and sounds, choose **Develop** from the tabs along the top of the main screen.*

■ *To view any virtual items purchased and any trade history, choose **Trade** from the menu bar down the left-hand side of the main screen, then go to **My Transactions**.*

*While the imagery on Roblox has a largely blocky, digitised look, parents should be aware that some of the user-generated games may include themes or imagery that may be too intense for young or sensitive players:*

■ *You can limit your child's account to display only a restricted list of available games to play. Go to **Settings**, select **Security** and turn on **Account Restrictions**.*

*Roblox players of all ages have their posts and chats filtered to prevent personal information from being shared, but no filter is foolproof. Roblox asks users and parents to report any inappropriate activity. Check your child's account and look to see if they have friends they do not know and talk to your child about what to report (including bullying, inappropriate behaviour or messages, scams and other game violations):*

■ *To report concerning behaviour on Roblox, players and parents can use the **Report Abuse** links located on game, group and user pages and in the **Report** tab of every game menu.*

■ *To block another player during a game session, find the user on the leaderboard/player list at the upper-right of the game screen. (If the leaderboard/player list isn't there, open it by clicking on your username in the upper-right corner.) From here, click on the player you wish to block and select **Block User**.*

**For further information and help, Roblox has created a parents' guide to the website which can be accessed at https://corp.roblox.com/parents**

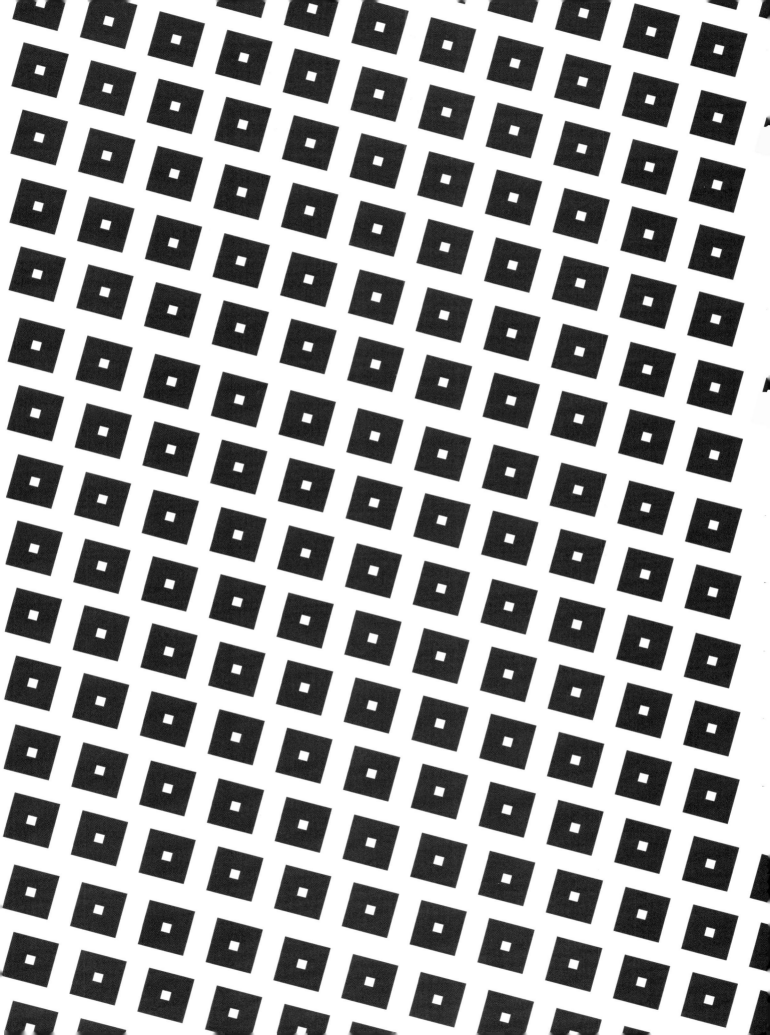

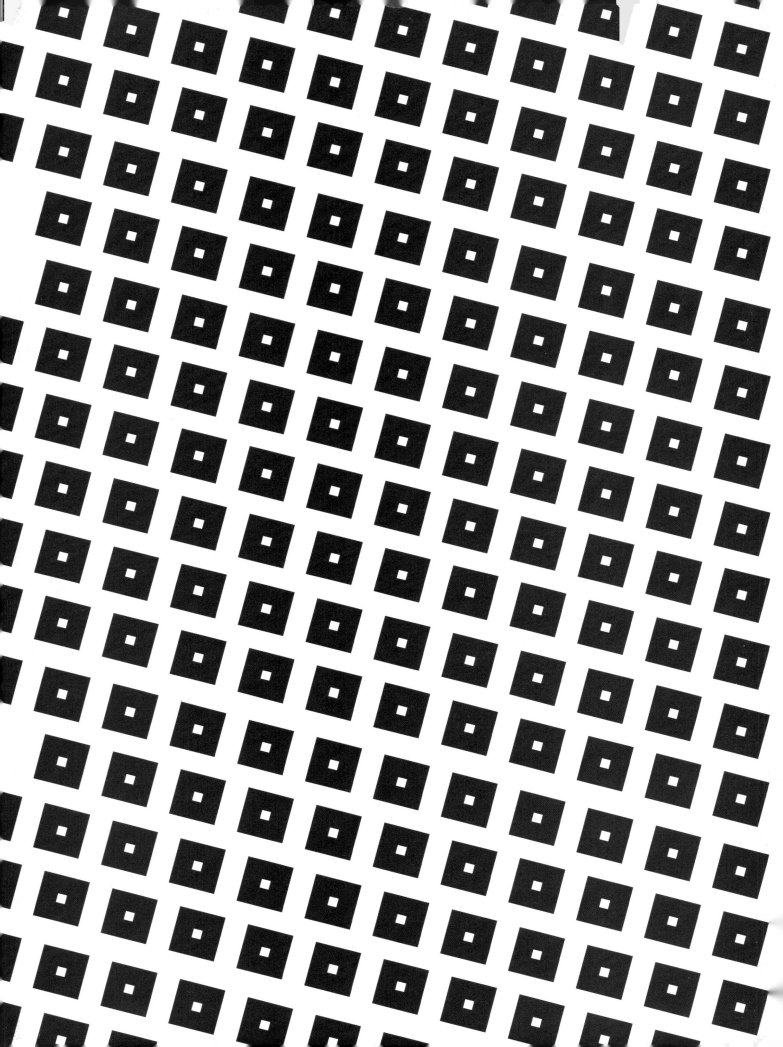